DON'T TOUCH THAT DIAL!
IT'S TIME TO PLAY . . .

THE OFFICIAL TV TRIVIA QUIZ

How well do you fare on the TV memory meter?
Tune in to this nostalgic new book, carefully created
to test your TV trivia quotient. Try your luck with
these sample channel challengers:

1. Who was Mayberry's lone telephone operator?
2. Can you identify *The Lone Ranger* theme song?
3. What TV powerhouse was the host of *Jackpot Bowling*?
4. Who played Lucy's friend, Caroline Appleby?
5. What was Pete and Gladys' last name?
6. State *My Mother, the Car*'s license plate number.

Answers are upside down below. If you answered
all of them correctly, you're a TV trivia wizard! If
not, hold on to your horizontal, get a good grip on
your vertical, and tackle the quizzes inside.

Bart Andrews is a TV comedy writer, playwright (co-
author of the musical *Ape Over Broadway*), magazine
journalist, and author of a new book about "I Love Lucy"
—*LUCY AND RICKY AND FRED AND ETHEL.*

1. Sarah
2. William Tell Overture
3. Milton Berle
4. Doris Singleton
5. Porter
6. PZR 317

Other SIGNET Puzzle Books You'll Enjoy

THE
OFFICIAL
TV TRIVIA
QUIZ BOOK #2

1,001 Boob-Tube Teasers for Media Maniacs

---

by
Bart Andrews

A SIGNET BOOK
NEW AMERICAN LIBRARY
TIMES MIRROR

*For J. Bradley Dunning
whose addiction to TV, like mine,
is absolutely abnormal.*

NAL BOOKS ARE ALSO AVAILABLE AT DISCOUNTS IN BULK
QUANTITY FOR INDUSTRIAL OR SALES-PROMOTIONAL USE.
FOR DETAILS, WRITE TO PREMIUM MARKETING DIVISION,
NEW AMERICAN LIBRARY, INC., 1301 AVENUE OF THE
AMERICAS, NEW YORK, NEW YORK 10019.

SIGNET, SIGNET CLASSICS, MENTOR, PLUME AND MERIDIAN BOOKS
are published by The New American Library, Inc.,
1301 Avenue of the Americas, New York, New York 10019

FIRST SIGNET PRINTING, OCTOBER, 1976

1 2 3 4 5 6 7 8 9

PRINTED IN THE UNITED STATES OF AMERICA

Acknowledgments

I especially wish to thank Mommy and Daddy for buying our 12-inch RCA Victor TV set (Model T-120, Serial Number C1800047) on August 8, 1950, or this volume would be titled *The Official Radio Trivia Quiz Book*.

And for their assorted assistance, I would like to express my sincere gratitude to Rick Carl, Jim Christian, Jerry Ervin, Steven Charles Peel, Gino Rossi, Kathy Slattery, Tony Slez, Marc Sotkin, Sandra Stubblefield, and all the fans of Ludlow Porch.

Lastly, to the kid who asked me for my autograph in the lobby of the RCA building after my *To Tell the Truth* appearance last year—please return my pen (Box 727, Hollywood, California 90028).

BART ANDREWS

QUESTIONS

1. LUCILLE BALL

1. What two movies did Lucy and Desi Arnaz make during *I Love Lucy* vacations?
2. On *The Lucy Show*, who played the recurring role of Joan Brenner?
3. Who played Lucy Carmichael's next door neighbor Harry?
4. On what ship did the Ricardos and the Mertzes travel to Europe in 1956?
5. What was Mr. Mooney's wife's first name?
6. Who played Caroline Appleby?
7. Can you recall the names of the three original writers of *I Love Lucy?*
8. Who was Fred Mertz's old vaudeville partner?
9. Eleven-year-old Ralph Hart portrayed Vivian Vance's son in *The Lucy Show*. What was his TV name?
10. What was Lucy Carter's address?

2. MUSIC MEN

Match the boy-from-the-band with his TV employer.

1. Ray Bloch
2. Sammy Spear
3. Hugo Montenegro
4. Henry Mancini
5. Wilbur Hatch
6. Mitchell Ayres
7. David Rose
8. Peter Matz
9. Skitch Henderson
10. Ken Lane

a. Perry Como
b. Carol Burnett
c. Ed Sullivan
d. Dean Martin
e. Jackie Gleason
f. *I Dream of Jeannie*
g. Steve Allen
h. Red Skelton
i. *Mr. Lucky*
j. *I Love Lucy*

3. NETWORK NOSTALGIA: CBS

1. How did the network once indicate the telecast of a color program?
2. According to Palladin, why did he use a certain chess piece as his symbol?
3. What major manufacturer sponsored *The Edge of Night?*
4. Who replaced Edward R. Murrow during his one-year sabbatical in 1959-60?
5. Who played Dr. Joe Gannon in the pilot of *Medical Center?*
6. On what floor was Dr. Robert Hartley's office?
7. What was *Kojak's* full name?
8. Who created the CBS eye?
9. Name the two performers who remained in the *Mission: Impossible* cast for its entire seven-year run.
10. What important subsidiary character did Glenn Strange portray on *Gunsmoke?*

4. "THE ANDY GRIFFITH SHOW"

1. Who was Mayberry's lone telephone operator?
2. What role did Hope Summers play?
3. Pyle was not Goober's original name. Can you recall what it was?
4. Who portrayed rambunctious Ernest T. Bass?
5. What was Andy Taylor's middle name? Ditto Barney Fife.
6. Denver Pyle and a musical group called The Dillards played what rowdy Mayberry family?
7. What relationship did Wally have to Gomer and Goober?
8. Where did Andy, Opie, and Aunt Bee live?
9. Before Aunt Bee came on the scene, who was Andy and Opie's housekeeper?
10. What role did Elinor Donahue play in early episodes?

5. WIVES' TALES

1. What was Dr. Richard Kimball's deceased wife's name?
2. How did *Julia* become a widow?
3. What did *Trouble With Father, I Love Lucy, Mr. Adams and Eve,* and *He and She* have in common?
4. Who was David Toma's wife?
5. What did Claudette Nevins and Lee Meriwether have in common in 1970?
6. Nanette Fabray played whose wife on her sitcom in the early sixties?
7. Lee Patrick and Anne Jeffreys played the wives on this comedy series. Name it.
8. Who portrayed the *Occasional Wife?*
9. Name George Jetson's wife.
10. With what TV comedian would you most associate Abby Dalton?

6. WHO'S WHO?

Match the actor with the character he portrayed and then identify the program.

1. Roy Roberts
2. Pat Harrington
3. Thurston Hall
4. George Chandler
5. Robert Lowery
6. Ben Alexander
7. Bob Sweeney
8. Frank Nelson
9. Johnny Lee
10. Joe Sawyer

a. Uncle Petrie
b. Oliver Munsey
c. Captain Huxley
d. Biff O'Hara
e. Algonquin J. Calhoun
f. Guido Panzini
g. Ralph Ramsey
h. Frank Smith
i. Tim Champion
j. Mr. Schuyler

7. "MY THREE SONS"

1. What was Bub's full name and who played the part?
2. Name the three boys who played the original three sons.
3. Whom did Robbie marry?
4. When Steve Douglas married a widow in 1970, he acquired a stepdaughter. Who played her?
5. With what musical instrument would you associate Fred MacMurray?
6. What was William Demarest's role?
7. How many children did Robbie and Katie have?
8. What two regulars were real-life brothers?
9. Who headed the production company responsible for the series?
10. Two networks carried the sitcom at various times. Name them.

8. SPORTS PAGE

1. With what sport would you associate Dennis James?
2. Who shared play-by-play chores on baseball's *Game of the Week?*
3. What network carries *The Wide World of Sports?*
4. The game of bridge was taught by what aficionado?
5. Who hosted *American Horse and Horseman?*
6. What sports-related job did Don Dunphy hold?
7. Bill the (Pabst) Bartender was portrayed by what well-known TV announcer?
8. What year were the Olympic Games first telecast?
9. Marty Glickman, whose specialty is basketball play-by-play, was once a professional athlete. What was his area of prowess?
10. With what sport would you associate Hatpin Mary?

9. CARTOON CORNER

1. Crusader Rabbit and Rags the Tiger lived where?
2. With what show would you associate Kurward Derby?
3. The character Dirty John was featured on what popular kiddie show?
4. What animated character worked for Spacely Sprockets?
5. Archie, Jughead, Reggie, Betty, and Veronica attended what school?
6. Who was the pesky neighbor of Huddles and Bubba, two football players?
7. What was the secret identity of Shoe Shine Boy?
8. Name Josie's two pussycats.
9. What Terrytoon featured two blackbirds?
10. What female did Snidely Whiplash and Dudley Do-Right pursue?

10. WHICH ONE DOESN'T BELONG?

From each group, select one entry which should not be included and explain why.

1. a) Sheriff Deadeye, b) The Mad Professor, c) Cauliflower McPugg, d) J. Newton Numskull, e) Willie Lump Lump

2. a) Gene Rayburn, b) Doc Severinsen, c) Hugh Downs, d) Milton DeLugg, e) Jose Melis

3. a) Peter Falk, b) James Whitmore, c) Chuck Connors, d) Burl Ives, e) William Windom

4. a) Roger Healey, b) Dwayne Doberman, c) Max Brodsky, d) Simon Butcher, e) Radar O'Reilly

5. a) Bette Davis, b) David Niven, c) Jane Powell, d) Charles Boyer, e) Jack Lemmon

6. a) *Marcus Welby, M.D.,* b) *The Defenders,* c) *Combat!,* d) *The Law of the Plainsman,* e) *Bonanza*

7. a) Lee Tracy, b) Lee Bowman, c) Hugh Marlow, d) Lee Philips, e) Jim Hutton

8. a) Grover, b) Sherlock Hemlock, c) Ernie, d) Flirt, e) Roosevelt Franklin

9. a) *The Gene Autry Show,* b) *Annie Oakley,* c) *The Range Rider,* d) *Champion,* e) *Black Saddle*

(Continued on page 11.)

11. AND NOW A WORD . . .

Match the announcer or narrator with the show or star.

1. Fred Foy
2. Rod Serling
3. George Fenneman
4. Don Wilson
5. William Conrad
6. Earl Hamner, Jr.
7. Bob Warren
8. Frank Gallop
9. Andre Baruch
10. Dave Garroway

a. *Wide, Wide World*
b. *Your Hit Parade*
c. *Twilight Zone*
d. *The Waltons*
e. Dick Cavett
f. Ralph Edwards
g. *You Bet Your Life*
h. *The Fugitive*
i. Perry Como
j. Jack Benny

(Continued from page 10.)
10. a) *Richard Diamond, Private Detective,* b) *The Mothers-In-Law,* c) *The Doris Day Show,* d) *The Streets of San Francisco,* e) *Your Show of Shows*

12. BASED ON THE MOVIE

Fill in the corresponding missing person in each foursome, and name the movie/TV series in which both pairs appeared.

1. Preston Foster is to Roddy McDowall as Gene Evans is to_____.
2. Irene Dunne is to_____as Peggy Wood is to Rosemary Rice.
3. Yul Brynner is to Deborah Kerr as _____ is to Samantha Eggar.
4. Spencer Tracy is to Joan Bennett as _____is to Ruth Warrick.
5. Arthur Lake is to Penny Singleton as Will Hutchins is to_____.
6. Tatum O'Neal is to Ryan O'Neal as Jodie Foster is to_____.
7. Elliot Gould is to Donald Sutherland as _____is to Alan Alda.
8. Johnny Sheffield is to Johnny Weissmuller as_____is to Ron Ely.
9. Lee Aaker is to John Wayne as Buddy Foster is to_____.
10. Alan Ladd is to Brandon de Wilde as _____is to Chris Shea.

13. TV FIRSTS

1. Who was the first to sign Carol Burnett's scrapbook in 1967?
2. Name the first film aired on *Saturday Night at the Movies*.
3. On November 6, 1955, the first major motion picture was telecast on NBC. Name it.
4. Who moderated the first TV debate between Presidential candidates John F. Kennedy and Richard M. Nixon in 1960?
5. What TV series version of a hit play was airing at the same time the play was running in New York?
6. Name the first Miss America to be crowned on television.
7. Which U.S. President was the first to appear on *Meet the Press?*
8. Name the first movie made especially for television.
9. What was NBC's first commercial broadcast (July, 1941)?
10. Who was the first President to televise a news conference?

14. "BONANZA"

1. What guitar player rendered the catchy theme song?
2. The long-running series didn't always air on Sunday. On what night did it originally appear?
3. What town was closest to the Ponderosa?
4. How many seasons did the oater run?
5. What part did young Mitch Vogel play?
6. Before becoming a rancher, Ben Cartwright had two other occupations. Name them.
7. What did Adam study in college?
8. Which *Bonanza* star was once a radio news-caster in Canada?
9. Who was the original sponsor of the show?
10. How many years did Pernell Roberts remain a member of the Cartwrights?

15. AROUND THE WORLD

1. In Spanish-speaking countries it's called *La Ley Del Revolver*. What is it better known to Americans as?
2. Where was *Maya* set?
3. Who portrayed Charlie Chan's Number One Son?
4. Chuck Connors, Tom Nardini, Ronald Howard, and young Gerald Edwards were the leads. What was the program?
5. Who replaced Kay Medford as the "housekeeper" on *To Rome With Love?*
6. John Russell and Chick Chandler teamed for two years to play footloose adventurers. Name the series.
7. The title role of *Richard the Lion Heart* was essayed by what dashing actor?
8. Who played an adventurous seafarer named Colin Glencannon?
9. In what part of the world did *Biff Baker, U.S.A.* take place?
10. Who was the female star of *Assignment—Foreign Legion?*

16. IT'S A DOG'S LIFE

Match the canine character with the show in which he romped.

1. Scruffy   a. *Chase*
2. Waldo   b. *Longstreet*
3. Fremont   c. *Sergeant Preston of the Yukon*
4. Lord Nelson   d. *The Ghost and Mrs. Muir*
5. Lad   e. *The Doris Day Show*
6. Bullet   f. *Please Don't Eat the Daisies*
7. Pax   g. *Nanny and the Professor*
8. King   h. *Dennis the Menace*
9. Tramp   i. *The Roy Rogers Show*
10. Fuzz   j. *My Three Sons*

17. WHAT . . .

1. . . . two towns did *Wyatt Earp* use as settings?
2. . . . sixties' musical show was hosted by Jack Linkletter?
3. . . . ex-football star was a regular on *Daniel Boone?*
4. . . . well-known TV producer once played Dr. Harvey Spencer Blair III on *Hennesey?*
5. . . . did *Empire,* the Richard Egan vehicle, refer to?
6. . . . was the original setting for *Mr. Lucky?*
7. . . . did Henry Phyfe do for a living?
8. . . . detective series, featuring Skip Homeier, was set on Hollywood's Sunset Strip?
9. . . . was the name of the series in which Vittorio de Sica was one of a quartet of stars?
10. . . . did Eddie Albert do for a living on *Leave It to Larry?*

18. WHAT'S WRONG?

In each capsulized description, there is one error. Find it and correct it.

1. The crew of the *PT 63* is on a mission to New Caledonia without Captain Binghamton's permission.
2. Dr. Zorba learns of Casey's intention to quit the neurological staff of Blair General.
3. Lucy and Ethel join the Thursday Afternoon Fine Arts League despite Ricky's attitude.
4. The Kramdens and the Nortons go to a convention of The Order of the Water Buffalo and one of them is voted Grand Pooh-Bah.
5. Jeff offends his buddy Chubby by calling Pokey a dumb mutt.
6. Eddie goes off on a camping trip with Uncle Norman, leaving his father alone with Miss Livingston.
7. Fury and his master Joey Norton disappear from the ranch without Jim or Pete knowing.
8. Aunt Harriet is arrested at the Gotham City Public Library by Chief Gordon for keeping a book over the two-week limit.
9. Marshal Dillon falls in love with Kitty Blake in a scheme to claim ownership of the Longbranch.
10. Mockingbird Flats is terrorized when Herman's father-in-law turns into a bat.

19. THE VOICE OF TELEVISION

Who provided the voices of these classic TV characters?

1. Cleo (*The People's Choice*)
2. Roger Ramjet
3. Cecil the Seasick Sea Serpent
4. Pebbles Flintstone
5. Judy Jetson
6. Oliver J. Dragon
7. Waldo (*Mr. Magoo*)
8. 1928 Porter (*My Mother, the Car*)
9. Sam (*Richard Diamond, Private Detective*)
10. Buster Brown

a. Mary Tyler Moore
b. Burr Tillstrom
c. Mary Jane Croft
d. Ed McConnell
e. Gary Owens
f. Sally Struthers
g. Janet Waldo
h. Stan Freberg
i. Jerry Hausner
j. Ann Sothern

20. "BEN CASEY"

1. What was Dr. Zorba's first name?
2. The series' opening film depicted five symbols being drawn on a blackboard. Name them in the proper order.
3. What was the name of the anesthesiologist?
4. Who played Dr. Ted Hoffman, Casey's cohort?
5. What two regulars were married in real life?
6. Who created the 1961 hospital drama?
7. What was Nick's last name?
8. On what night was the series first carried?
9. What famous movie actor owned the show?
10. Who was billed as technical advisor?

21. BLACK IS BEAUTIFUL

1. Who played Charlie, the elevator operator, on *My Little Margie?*
2. In what American city is *Good Times* set?
3. What did Pete Dixon teach at Walt Whitman High School?
4. Joe Mannix employed an extremely capable secretary. What was her full name and who played the role?
5. Of Jester Hairston, Horace Stewart, and Spencer Williams, who played the classic character, Lightnin'?
6. In what short-lived series did Harrison Page and Janet MacLachlan play a young married couple?
7. Who was the Hendersons' maid?
8. What was Greg Morris' role on *Mission: Impossible?*
9. Who was Don Adams' costar on *The Partners?*
10. Flip Wilson's character Geraldine has a last name. What is it?

22. MINOR MATCH

Match the juvenile performer with the TV series in which he or she was a featured player.

1. Mitch Vogel   a. *I Love Lucy*
2. Ronald Keith   b. *The Ed Wynn Show*
3. Mike Mayer   c. *It's About Time*
4. Steven Born   d. *Bonanza*
5. Pamelyn Ferdin   e. *The Lucy Show*
6. Pat Cardi   f. *The Great Gildersleeve*
7. Lisa Loring   g. *Happy*
8. Ralph Hart   h. *Please Don't Eat the Daisies*
9. Sherri Alberoni   i. *The Addams Family*
10. Brian Nash   j. *The Paul Lynde Show*

23. ED SULLIVAN

1. When did *The Toast of the Town* become *The Ed Sullivan Show?*
2. Fill in the missing word in the following Ed Sullivan philosophy: "Open big, have a good comedy act, put in something for ————— and keep the show clean."
3. What two songs did the Beatles sing on their first appearance in 1964?
4. Who was Sullivan's earliest sponsor?
5. How much did Ed pay Elvis for his first three appearances, the first of which was on September 9, 1956?
6. What do singer Monica Lewis, ballerina Kathryn Lee, fight referee Ruby Goldstein, and Rodgers and Hammerstein have in common?
7. How many consecutive years was Ed on the air?
8. What was Sullivan's wife's name?
9. Who was his long-standing commercial spokeswoman?
10. What do *The Bill Dana Show, The Travels of Jaimie McPheeters, National Velvet, Pete Kelly's Blues,* and *Branded* have in common?

24. QUOTE, UNQUOTE

With what TV show or personality would you associate the following expressions?
1. "You bet your bippy."
2. "Ya'll come back now, ya hear."
3. "We'll be ready to go in exactly thirty seconds."
4. "Is it bigger than a breadbox?"
5. "Abracadabra, please, and thank you."
6. *"¡Miraquetienecosalamujeresta!"*
7. "Good night and God bless."
8. "Will it be a hit or a miss?"
9. "I arrest you in the name of the Crown."
10. "Enter, whoever. If it's nobody, I'll call back."

25. HOLD YOUR HORSES!

1. Pat Conway
2. Charles Bateman
3. Peter Brown

4. Richard Carlson
5. Scott Brady
6. Clu Gulager
7. Peter Breck
8. Allen Case
9. Don Durant
10. Dack Rambo

a. *Tombstone Territory*
b. *The Tall Man*
c. *The Guns of Will Sonnett*
d. *Two Faces West*
e. *The Deputy*
f. *MacKenzie's Raiders*
g. *Johnny Ringo*
h. *Lawman*
i. *Shotgun Slade*
j. *Black Saddle*

26. TRUE OR FALSE?

1. *Search for Tomorrow* is the first daytime serial to celebrate its 25th anniversary on television.
2. George Burns played himself on *Wendy and Me*.
3. Ed McMahon played Clarabell.
4. Neil Brock was a Congressman's assistant.
5. Sal Mineo played the title role in *The Rebel*.
6. *Bracken's World* depicted life on a magazine.
7. Peter Kastner played the title role in *The Ugliest Girl in Town*.
8. *Ichabod and Me* was set in a sleepy upstate New York town.
9. *Kentucky Jones* was a veterinarian.
10. *Here We Go Again* was a show about divorce.

27. FRIENDS AND LOVERS

1. Who played Hazel's friend Rosie?
2. What role did Hal Buckley play on *O.K. Crackerby?*
3. Name the Italian woman who was a neighbor of the Kramdens and the Nortons.
4. Who portrayed Phyllis Pruitt's neighbor Regina Wentworth?
5. Where did Barney Fife's occasional girlfriend, Juanita, work?
6. Who played Vern Albright's girlfriend Roberta Townsend?
7. What role did X. Brands play on *Yancy Derringer?*
8. Chatsworth Osborne was his friend; Thalia Menninger was his lover. Who was it, and who played the three parts?
9. Who portrayed Socrates Miller's friend Rollo on *The People's Choice?* (Hint: He also played Schultzy's boyfriend on *The Bob Cummings Show.*)
10. Whose friend was Rockwell Sin?

28. LET'S PLAY GAMES

Identify the game show from these clues.
1. Provide the question to the answer given
2. Rebus
3. Impostors
4. Heartbreaking stories
5. Charades
6. Timed stunts
7. Tic-tac-toe
8. Win a houseful of furniture
9. A test of the senses
10. Celebrities disguised by ingenious makeup techniques

29. BOX OFFICE BABIES

Match the stars with their foreign birthplaces.

1. Jinx Falkenburg   a. Toronto, Canada
2. Wendy Barrie   b. Saskatchewan,
                                 Canada
3. John Daly   c. London, England
4. Nina Foch   d. Barcelona, Spain
5. Bob Hope   e. London, England
6. Beatrice Lillie   f. Hong Kong, China
7. Art Linkletter   g. Neath, Wales
8. Henny Youngman   h. Johannesburg, South
                                 Africa
9. Ray Milland   i. Eltham, England
10. Ida Lupino   j. Leyden, Holland

1. Who played Mr. Pomfritt, a *Dobie Gillis* character?
2. What was Lee Marvin's role in *M Squad?*
3. Sarah Green, Professor Crayton, Miss Maxfield, and Joe Caldwell were leading characters in what sixties sitcom?
4. Who lived on the *Fortuna,* a chic cabin cruiser?
5. In 1961, Edd Byrnes walked off *77 Sunset Strip* to be replaced briefly by what handsome actor?
6. Who played the recurring role of Doc Holliday on *Maverick?*
7. In what town was the *Bus Stop?*
8. Brian Kelly and John Ashley costarred in an adventure series about what exciting sport?
9. What well-known comedy duo shared star billing on *Holiday Lodge?*
10. Who hosted *International Showtime?*

31. "FATHER KNOWS BEST"

1. Who portrayed Bud's two buddies, Claude and Kippy?
2. Young Richard Eyer played Kathy's boyfriend a few times. What was the beau's name?
3. Can you recall Kitten's middle name?
4. Who was the Andersons' gardener?
5. After portraying Jim Anderson and before taking the Hippocratic oath as Marcus Welby, Robert Young played what character on what series?
6. What business was Margaret's father engaged in?
7. Was the series an adaptation of a movie, play, or radio series?
8. Who were the Andersons' next door neighbors?
9. What automobile manufacturer furnished the cars used on the show?
10. What was Bud's favorite sport?

1. Patty Duke and Anne Bancroft reprised their TV and stage roles in the film version of this real-life drama. Can you recall the former's role?
2. Who wrote *A Visit to a Small Planet?*
3. Cliff Robertson played it on TV and Jack Lemmon did the movie version, but Charles Bickford appeared in both versions. Name the property.
4. On which anthology series did *The Miracle Worker* make its first impact?
5. Who directed the TV and film versions of *Marty?*
6. Life inside a large corporation was depicted in this Rod Serling TV drama-then-movie. Name it.
7. Who inherited Thelma Ritter's role in the film version of *The Catered Affair?*
8. *Requiem For a Heavyweight* was the poignant story of a washed-up prizefighter. What was his name?
9. *Judgment at Nuremburg* had its origins as a 90-minute drama done on what anthology show?
10. Of Franchot Tone, Robert Cummings, Edward Arnold, Walter Abel, Paul Hartman, George Voskovec, John Beal, Lee Philips, Norman Fell, Joseph Sweeney, Bart Burns, and Will West, which two actors appeared in the movie version of *Twelve Angry Men?*

33. TV SCREEN TEST

Match the two characters played by the same performer; then identify the actor or actress.

1. Connie Brooks   a. Mrs. Banford
2. Liz Cooper   b. Leroy Simpson
3. Mrs. Gurney   c. Hoby Gilman
4. Kate Bradley   d. Liza Hammond
5. Sally Rogers   e. Terry Bowen
6. Matt Anders   f. Sally
7. Kelly Robinson   g. Blanche Morton
8. Hannibal Dobbs   h. Myrna Givens
9. Mr. Kaufman   i. Mr. Ellenhorn
10. Dennis Mitchell   j. Bill Davis

34. THE YEAR 1948

1. Who was the first moderator of *Meet the Press?*
2. Can you describe the original purpose of test patterns?
3. Do you remember who Tuffy Brasuhn was?
4. Within 10,000, how many TV sets existed at the end of the year?
5. Who was the host of *The Camel News Caravan?*
6. What yearly sporting event was televised for the first time in '48?
7. Sing the first eight bars of the *Howdy Doody* theme song.
8. According to the Lone Ranger, what was "a symbol that means justice and law"?
9. Who hosted *Juvenile Jury?*
10. What was the name of Hopalong Cassidy's steed?

35. THE YEAR 1949

1. What performer had two separate TV series running simultaneously, both bearing his name in the title?
2. What famous playwright appeared as a regular panelist on *This Is Show Business?*
3. Who was the first Negro to have his own TV show?
4. What network carried *Captain Video?*
5. Cliffy, Scampy, and Nicky were the clowns on this Sealtest-sponsored program. Name it.
6. What zany comedy team starred in *Fireball Fun For All?*
7. To whom did *Easy Aces* refer?
8. What type of show did Dione Lucas pioneer?
9. What was the original title of *Your Show of Shows?*
10. Who conducted the NBC Symphony on a '49 special?

1. What thrice-weekly program closed with the following narration: "Don't miss the next action-packed episode, when the space cadets are faced with new, mysterious dangers in their exploration of the planet never before seen by earth mortals"?
2. El Squeako, Gala Poochie, and Mr. Deetle Dootle were characters on what popular program?
3. With what cigarette would you associate Perry Como?
4. Louis Untermeyer, Harold Hoffman, Arlene Francis, and Dr. Richard Hoffman were the first panelists on what game show?
5. Who made his NBC television debut on Easter Sunday? (Hint: He sang "Baby, It's Cold Outside" with Dinah Shore.)
6. Denise Lor and Ken Carson were favorites on whose daytime variety series?
7. Dagmar (Virginia Ruth Egnor) of *Broadway Open House* fame hails from what state?
8. In what Los Angeles department store did Jack Benny meet Mary Livingston?
9. Who hosted *Truth or Consequences*?
10. What did *Big Town* and *I Cover Times Square* have in common?

37. THE YEAR 1951

1. Characters in what comedy series belonged to The Mystic Knights of the Sea Lodge?
2. Who created *Truth or Consequences?*
3. What did Stu Erwin do for a living on *Trouble With Father?*
4. Everyone knows that *The Cisco Kid*'s horse was Diablo, but what was Pancho's steed named?
5. What did Marilyn Monroe and Dennis Day have in common?
6. Who preceded Audrey Peters as Vanessa on *Love of Life?*
7. How old was Lucille Ball when she started *I Love Lucy?*
8. Who composed Ernie Kovacs' theme song?
9. What was Reed Hadley's role on *Racket Squad?*
10. The panelists were Carmelita Pope, Toni Gilman, Robert Breen, and Francis Coughlin; the moderator was Bergen Evans. Name the game.

38. THE YEAR 1952

1. Who composed the original musical score for *Victory at Sea?*
2. What was the year's Number One song on *Your Hit Parade?*
3. Jim Backus played a judge of what court on *I Married Joan?*
4. What situation comedy that began this year went on to become the longest-running in its genre?
5. Where did the Albrights of *My Little Margie* live?
6. Before commercial sponsorship, who backed *Omnibus?*
7. Bones and Stretch were cousins, and students of *Our Miss Brooks.* What last name did they share?
8. Name *The Lone Ranger* theme song.
9. Of Darby, Doc, and Thorny, which *Ozzie and Harriet* character did Parley Baer portray?
10. For whom did Millie (*Meet Millie*) work as a secretary?

39. THE YEAR 1953

1. CBS and NBC both carried this special, which featured Mary Martin and Ethel Merman. Name it.
2. In what section of New York was *Marty* set?
3. Who was *Topper*'s maid?
4. What was *Mr. Peeper*'s first name?
5. Pupi Campo led the band for whose morning variety show?
6. What did *Saturday Night Revue* and *Laramie* have in common?
7. Which actor or actress on *The Guiding Light* used his or her own last name on the show?
8. Who hosted *My Favorite Story*?
9. What two actresses played the maid Louise on *Make Room for Daddy*?
10. Whose radio role did Joan Caulfield inherit?

1. Fill in the missing lyrics in "Ballad of Davy Crockett": "Born on a mountaintop in ——/Greenest —— in the Land of the Free/—— in the woods so's he knew ev'ry tree/Kilt him a —— when he was only three/Davy, Davy Crockett, King of the wild —— !"
2. What were J. C. Dithers' first and middle names on *Blondie?*
3. Who starred in TV's first "spectacular," *Satins and Spurs?*
4. When Walt Disney first came to television, what was the title of his show?
5. What was the name of the central family on *The Secret Storm?*
6. Who played Corliss Archer's father?
7. On *People Are Funny,* what was the word-scramble game called?
8. What was the full name of the juvenile character on *Rin Tin Tin?*
9. Who essayed the title role in *The Files of Jeffrey Jones?*
10. What was Verna Felton's full character name on *December Bride?*

41. THE YEAR 1955

1. What was the title of the daily afternoon drama anthology?
2. An official of what bank guarded the questions and prize money on *The $64,000 Question?*
3. What city job did Throckmorton P. Gildersleeve hold?
4. How large was *The Millionaire*'s estate?
5. Whom did Mayor John Peoples marry?
6. What brand of watch was thrown over Niagara Falls in an early commercial?
7. Where does *Captain Kangaroo* reside?
8. What two roles did Cyril Ritchard play in *Peter Pan?*
9. Crew-cutted Rocky Rockwell was a trumpeteer in whose TV band?
10. What classic singer's TV debut occurred on *Ford Star Jubilee?*

42. THE YEAR 1956

1. What was the title of the Joseph Cotten-hosted series based on authentic court cases?
2. Name the famous comedy team who made their last appearance before parting company in '56.
3. Where was *Stanley* set?
4. Bimbo the Elephant was featured on what series?
5. What two newsmen joined forces this year to form a team?
6. What was Gale Storm's full name on *Oh! Susanna?*
7. Who was the highest-paid commercial spokeswoman on TV this year?
8. Name *Annie Oakley*'s boyfriend.
9. With what long-running soap opera would you associate Santos Ortega?
10. Who was the host of *Zane Grey Theater?*

1. What locally televised teen-age dance-athon graduated to network status?
2. Who sang the *Have Gun, Will Travel* theme song?
3. Name *Zorro*'s "deaf-mute" friend.
4. Rob, Nell, Ken, and Gus were the main characters of what series based on a novel by Mary O'Hara?
5. What super-popular situation comedy revamped its format by doing hour-long specials?
6. On *Bachelor Father,* who was Peter's oft-mentioned cousin?
7. Who played Pepino Garcia on *The Real McCoys?*
8. For what major league baseball team did the star of *The Rifleman* once play?
9. What was the name of the tiny clay hero who had his own show?
10. The "does-she-or-doesn't-she" advertising slogan referred to what product?

1. Within $50,000, how much did game-show contestant Teddy Nadler win?
2. On what program did Carroll O'Connor portray a blacksmith?
3. Who called his gun "Mare's Laig"?
4. What series involved three Civil War veterans in search of a new life in the West?
5. Who was the host of the short-lived *ESP* series?
6. What nightclub did *Peter Gunn* frequent?
7. *Life With Elizabeth* and *A Date With the Angels* shared what actress in the starring roles?
8. Who were the co-hosts of *Brains and Brawn*?
9. What comic-strip character did Dean Fredericks bring to video life?
10. Who played John Beamer on *The Ed Wynn Show?*

45. THE YEAR 1959

1. On what show did Fidel Castro appear on April 19th?
2. Where did *Staccato,* starring John Cassavetes, take place?
3. Who played Grey Holden on *Riverboat?*
4. What was the title of the first *Twilight Zone* episode?
5. Who starred as Lt. Ben Guthrie in *Lineup?*
6. Who played John Wilson's wife?
7. In what series did these actors—then unknowns—appear: Peter Falk, Mike Connors, Jack Klugman, Telly Savalas, Lee Marvin, Robert Redford, Charles Bronson, Cliff Robertson, Ricardo Montalban, and Frank Gorshin?
8. What role did Jeannie Russell essay on *Dennis the Menace?*
9. Johnny Russo, Steve Nelson, and Chris Ballard were cop characters on this series. Name it.
10. What role did Hal Peary play on *Fibber McGee and Molly?*

46. THE YEAR 1960

1. What was *Pete and Gladys'* last name?
2. The cast included Troy Donahue, Diane McBain, Van Williams, and Lee Patterson. Name the series.
3. A joke about what "sensitive" subject drove Jack Paar temporarily off the air?
4. What famous husband-and-wife team was divorced?
5. Bea Benadaret provided the voice for what *Flintstones* character?
6. What TV powerhouse became the host of *Jackpot Bowling?*
7. New York's 65th Precinct was the setting for what police drama?
8. On what comedy did Ronnie Burns play the father of an "outspoken" infant?
9. Who hosted *Thriller?*
10. What did *Angel* and *I Love Lucy* have in common?

1. What breed was *Mr. Ed?*
2. Bob Carson, Hank Gogerty, and Lionel were characters on whose sitcom?
3. What was *Dr. Kildare*'s first name?
4. Gunther and Francis were the first names of what comic duo of flatfoots? Also, name the series.
5. Who played attorney Abraham Lincoln Jones?
6. What *Sing Along With Mitch* regular would later find fame on *Sesame Street?*
7. Who was the "fastest left-handed gun in the West"?
8. Larry Pennell and Ken Curtis played sky divers in this Ivan Tors production. Name it.
9. What roles did E. G. Marshall and Robert Reed play on *The Defenders?*
10. Name two series in which James Franciscus played an insurance investigator.

48. THE YEAR 1962

1. What was Owen Wister better known as?
2. Name the ship on *Ensign O'Toole*.
3. Comic carpenters, Harry and Arch, were better known by other names. What were they?
4. What New York police precinct did Toody, Muldoon, and Schnauzer cover on their beat?
5. Warren Oates, Bruce Dern, and Robert Dowdell were his Western costars. Who is he?
6. What was the name of the military academy featured on *McKeever and the Colonel?*
7. For whom did *Our Man Higgins* serve as butler?
8. Hale, Hawks, Charley, and Duke were characters on what program?
9. Who was the host of the music series *The Lively Ones?*
10. What setting did *Combat!* and *The Gallant Men* share?

1. Who played Patty Lane's brother Ross on *The Patty Duke Show?*
2. What hotel was the home of the Bradleys of *Petticoat Junction?*
3. Who replaced Dean Jagger as principal of Jefferson High School on *Mr. Novak?*
4. Who was paid $250,000 to conduct a TV tour of London?
5. Maggie Fielding, Matt Powers, Althea Davis, and Brock Hayden were characters in what Emmy Award-winning soap opera?
6. Who was Minnesota Congressman Glen Morley's assistant?
7. He played Doc on *The Travels of Jaimie McPheeters.* Name the actor.
8. North Fork was the setting for what popular Western?
9. Who were *Harry's Girls?*
10. Glynis Johns and Keith Andes played husband and wife on *Glynis.* What was the couple's last name?

50. THE YEAR 1964

1. Who portrayed Marion Butnick on *Broadside?*
2. What was Gomez Addams' profession?
3. His costars were Alejandro Rey, Kathie Browne, and Francine York in this politically oriented series. Name the star and the show.
4. Who created *Another World?*
5. What did the initials in *The Man from U.N.C.L.E.* stand for?
6. What did T.H.R.U.S.H. mean?
7. Who were *The Rogues?*
8. Where did Herman Munster work?
9. Who played PR man Mike Bell, and what was the name of the show?
10. Name the series in which a family named Ricks appeared.

1. What California license plate number belonged to the 1928 Porter, star of *My Mother, the Car?*

2. Originally, how many years did Paul Bryan (*Run For Your Life*) have to live?

3. Artemus Gordon and Jim West were government agents on what series?

4. Who produced *I Spy?*

5. Young Joe and Jeff Fithian played twins on what popular comedy?

6. *Green Acres* shared its setting with what other bucolic comedy?

7. What company urged us to put a "tiger" in our tanks?

8. Greg Garrison produced a successful show for what movie star?

9. Who replaced Ivan Dixon in the cast of *Hogan's Heroes?*

10. What delightful TV character made her exits exclaiming, "toodles"?

52. THE YEAR 1966

1. On what series did the late martial artist, Bruce Lee, play a supporting role?
2. Where did the Pruitts live?
3. Robert Loggia starred in *T.H.E. Cat.* What did the abbreviation stand for?
4. What two Chuck Barris game shows debuted this year?
5. On what ABC series was *The Love Song of Barney Kempinski* presented?
6. Complete this *Mission: Impossible* staple: "This tape will self-destruct in ——."
7. What U.S. Senator performed on *The Hollywood Palace*?
8. Who played Ann Sheridan's mother on *Pistols 'n' Petticoats*?
9. What soap opera was set partially at University Hospital?
10. On what series did a character named Miss Faversham appear?

1. Name the twins born to Jerry and Suzie on *The Mothers-In-Law*.
2. Did Jack Cassidy play Oscar North or Jetman on *He and She*?
3. What is *Ironside*'s full name?
4. Who played Joe Mannix's agency boss during the first season of the detective series?
5. On whose short-lived variety show did Dick Curtis, Abby Dalton, Charlie Weaver, and Stan Ross play a bunch of second bananas?
6. In what western town did Stuart Whitman play Marshal Jim Crown?
7. Did *Captain Nice* take a pill or a potion to become a crime fighter?
8. Who essayed the role of George Armstrong Custer?
9. Where did Sisters Bertrille and Jacqueline live?
10. What series boasted a 650-pound star in the title role?

54. THE YEAR 1968

1. What soap opera was the first to explore ethnic intermarriage?
2. Who played Mike Jones' friend Harold?
3. What popular variety show host was born in Delight, Arkansas?
4. Name the two magazines which Dan Farrell and Jeff Dillon edited on *Name of the Game*.
5. Where did Doris Martin's father Buck live?
6. Who played the elder nurse associate of *Julia*'s?
7. What was Hugh Hefner's variety-interview show called?
8. Whose variety show featured a weekly segment spoofing United States Presidents?
9. Where was *Lancer* set?
10. Who wrote the original *Laugh-In* songs?

55. THE YEAR 1969

1. What was motorcyclist Bronson's first name?
2. Who played Lana Turner's son on *The Survivors?*
3. Jack Wild played what *H.R. Pufnstuf* role?
4. What Academy Award-winner was in *The Courtship of Eddie's Father?*
5. Who created *Marcus Welby, M.D.?*
6. What was Carol's last name before she joined *The Brady Bunch?*
7. Julie Barnes, Pete Cochran, and Linc Hayes were *The Mod Squad.* Who was their mentor?
8. What project cost ABC $16 million this year?
9. Besides being a surgeon at University Medical Center, what was Dr. Gannon's other responsibility?
10. Tom Bosley, Patricia Smith, Bobby Rhia, and Don Chastain were her costars. Name the sitcom.

1. From what New Mexico town did *McCloud* hail?
2. Who played Mary Richards' parents?
3. "Come On, Get Happy" was the theme song for what musical sitcom?
4. What was the theme song of *Headmaster?*
5. Lancelot Link, the Simian spy, worked for A.P.E. What did these initials stand for?
6. Who played Danny Thomas' six-year-old grandson?
7. What famous newsman retired from television?
8. To what did *Paris 7000* refer?
9. Name the two performers who repeated their *Odd Couple* movie roles in the TV version.
10. Celeste Holm, John Fink, and Robert F. Simon were Renne Jarrett's costars in this situation comedy about the First Family. Name it.

1. Who played Clark Kent's *Daily Planet* editor, Perry White?

2. Who was Richard Diamond's telephone answering service go-between?

3. Name the two actors who played Blanche Morton's husband.

4. Whom did Ben Alexander portray on the original *Dragnet* series?

5. Of *Name That Tune, I've Got a Secret, Where Was I?, Masquerade Party,* and *The Price Is Right,* with which one was Bill Cullen *not* associated?

6. Which network carried these Western heroes?

7. What was Emmett Clark's wife's name, and who played her?

8. Who portrayed *The Munsters'* niece Marilyn?

9. Who was Phineas T. Bluster's twin brother?

10. What is this piano virtuoso's full name?

57. THE YEAR 1971

1. On *Funny Face,* Sandy hailed from Tyler, Texas. According to a scene in the opening film, what was this town's population?
2. Ruth Warrick and Hugh Franklin played what two characters on *All My Children?*
3. Who played the star of the fictional, Phoenix-based *Dick Preston Show?*
4. Wes Stern and Bobby Sherman played a pair of rock songwriters on what program?
5. Who played cooking "expert" Julia Grown-up?
6. Joan Darling played Frieda Krause on what show?
7. Link McCray, Uncle Lazlo, and Nick Marco were characters on what period sitcom?
8. Who was the host of *Stand Up and Cheer?*
9. For whom did Larry Hagman and Donna Mills work as butler and cook on *The Good Life?*
10. Who played *Monty Nash?*

58. THE YEAR 1972

1. What is the number of the *M*A*S*H* unit?
2. Who played the youthful Caine (Grasshopper) on *Kung Fu?*
3. What was Vivian Harmon's maiden name?
4. How many Loud children were profiled in PBS' *An American Family?*
5. What is the number of the Los Angeles County rescue facility featured on *Emergency?*
6. What actress played the go-between in *The Delphi Bureau?*
7. Robert Forster and Joan Blondell starred in what detective series set in the thirties?
8. What was the original title of NBC's *Circle of Fear?*
9. Jane Actman and John Calvin portrayed newlyweds on what Santa Barbara-set series?
10. Who played *Banacek*'s girlfriend?

59. THE YEAR 1973

1. Lockwood, Bianco, Grover, Cameron, and Harding were characters in what short-lived series?
2. What was the American version of the British-originated *On the Buses?*
3. Who moved into David and Ricky Nelson's bedroom when Ozzie and Harriet returned to television?
4. Who played nightclub owner Pierre Rolland on *The Young and the Restless?*
5. What was the setting for *Roll Out!?*
6. What were the *Snoop Sisters'* first names?
7. How long did *Faraday* spend in a South American jungle prison?
8. What was Doc Elliot's first name?
9. Who portrayed Anthony Dorian?
10. Who was *Adam's Rib?*

60. THE YEAR 1974

1. Name *Baretta*'s cockatoo.
2. What Martin Caidin novel was the basis for *The Six Million Dollar Man?*
3. Can you recall Rhoda's New York address?
4. Who played Dr. Julie Franklin on *How to Survive a Marriage?*
5. What did Richie Cunningham's father do for a living?
6. Which *Planet of the Apes* star made the transition from movies to television?
7. How many children did Zack Wheeler have?
8. For what news syndicate did Carl Kolchak write?
9. Where did Lucas Tanner teach?
10. During what period was *Manhunter* set?

61. THE YEAR 1975

1. What *Good Times* star wrote the theme song for *The Jeffersons?*
2. At what school was *Welcome Back Kotter* set?
3. Name the recent film on which *Switch* was loosely based.
4. *Joe Forrester* was a spin-off of what other TV series?
5. Who originally played Julie Erskine on *Phyllis?*
6. Before *On the Rocks,* Jose Perez costarred in a CBS sitcom set in New York. Name it.
7. Before reteaming with his ex-wife, Sonny Bono had his own variety show. What was its title?
8. What did the *Three for the Road* family call their motor-home?
9. Which character on the TV version of *The Swiss Family Robinson* was not a creation of Daniel Defoe?
10. At what TV station did Peter Campbell work?

62. WHERE DOES IT HURT?

Match the doctor character with the actor who portrayed him, and name the program.

1. Dr. Konrad Styner
2. Dr. Hudson
3. Dr. Christian
4. Dr. Michael Rossi
5. Dr. McKinley
   Thompson
6. Dr. Sean Jamison
7. Dr. Matt Lincoln
8. Dr. Ted Steffen
9. Dr. Theodore
   Bassett
10. Dr. Peter Goldstone

a. Vince Edwards
b. Brian Keith
c. Broderick Crawford
d. Richard Boone

e. Paul Richards
f. John Howard
g. Wendell Corey
h. Macdonald Carey

i. Ed Nelson
j. Joseph Campanella

63. NETWORK NOSTALGIA: NBC

1. Can you describe the network's first commercial?
2. When did the network introduce "living color"?
3. In June, 1936, RCA opened its first TV "sending" station. Where was it located?
4. What was *Another World*'s companion soap when it debuted?
5. On what two sitcoms did Ernest Truex and Sylvia Field play the parents of leading characters?
6. Micah Torrence was the sheriff on what half-hour Western?
7. What made *The Wackiest Ship in the Army* different from other situation comedies?
8. Emmett Ryker and Henry Garth were Western characters on what classic oater?
9. Who created the *Today* format?
10. What locale did *Karen; Tom, Dick and Mary;* and *Harris Against the World* have in common?

64. VIDEO CLUES

Which stars do the following clues bring to mind?
1. A necklace with a diamond heart on it.
2. "The Singing Rage."
3. Gonzaga University.
4. A hand cupped over one ear.
5. Piano-shaped swimming pool.
6. "Mwah."
7. "The Cracker-Barrel Socrates."
8. "Songbird of the South."
9. "Glad we could get together."
10. A tug on the earlobe.

65. "ALL IN THE FAMILY"

1. What is the Bunkers' address?
2. Name several of Archie Bunker's neighbors.
3. Who wrote the lyrics to the "Remembering You" closing theme?
4. What former "Dead End Kid" appears regularly as one of Archie's cronies?
5. Name the actor who plays Kelcy.
6. Who is Archie and Edith's grandson?
7. What relationship is Maude Findlay to the Bunkers?
8. Who is the Bunkers' minister?
9. On what BBC program is the show based?
10. "Dead from the neck up" defines what classic Archie-ism?

66. SET SURVEY

According to a 1975 survey, there are 264 million black and white TV sets in the world. See if you can match the Top Ten nations with the number of sets in use in each case.

		(millions)	
1.	Spain	a.	12
2.	Russia	b.	5.7
3.	West Germany	c.	63.4
4.	Japan	d.	50
5.	Canada	e.	5.7
6.	Italy	f.	8.5
7.	Brazil	g.	12.45
8.	France	h.	13.25
9.	U.S.A.	i.	10.9
10.	United Kingdom	j.	6.12

67. WOMEN'S PAGE

Arrange the following programs in the proper chronological order, according to the year they began.

1. *I Married Joan*
2. *My Little Margie*
3. *I Love Lucy*
4. *A Touch of Grace*
5. *My Sister Eileen*
6. *Karen*
7. *I Dream of Jeannie*
8. *Glynis*
9. *Dear Phoebe*
10. *Mrs. G. Goes to College*

68. "LEAVE IT TO BEAVER"

1. Where did the Cleavers live?
2. Other than "Theodore," what did Eddie Haskell call the Beaver?
3. Who was Beaver's teacher and who was the school principal?
4. What role did Burt Mustin play?
5. What was Whitey's last name?
6. Where did Beaver attend school?
7. Who played Gilbert Bates?
8. How long did the series run?
9. What memorable role did little Joey Scott portray?
10. Who played "Lumpy" Rutherford?

69. WHO'S WHO?

Match the actress with the character she portrayed and then identify the program.

1. Ann McCrea   a. Tugboat Annie
2. Hope Emerson   b. Della Street
3. Minerva Urecal   c. Shirley Balukis
4. Elizabeth Baur   d. Ellen Monroe
5. Susan St. James   e. Midge Kelsey
6. Barbara Hale   f. Sylvia Caldwell
7. Diana Muldaur   g. Sarge
8. Eleanor Parker   h. Joy Adamson
9. Joan Hotchkis   i. Peggy Maxwell
10. Candy Azzara   j. Teresa O'Brien

70. JACKIE GLEASON

1. Who played Jackie's wife on *The Life of Riley?*
2. What was the bevy of beautiful girls called on *The American Scene Magazine?*
3. Who played Crazy Guggenheim?
4. Can you remember Alice's punchline to this classic dialogue exchange? Alice: "Look, Ralph, maybe I could get a job to help out." Ralph: "Oh, no, you don't. When I married you, I promised you'd never have to work again." Alice: "But it won't be for long." Ralph: "I don't care, Alice. I've got my pride. Before I'd let you go to work. I'd rather see you starve. We'll just have to live on our savings."
5. Who was Stanley R. Soog?
6. Who was The Great One's female foil when he returned to the medium in 1962?
7. In what part of New York City did the Kramdens and the Nortons reside?
8. Who choreographed Gleason's TV shows?
9. On *The Honeymooners,* who played Ralph's mother-in-law (by coincidence, she was the original Alice Kramden)?
10. Where, other than New York, has Jackie mounted his television shows?

71. "THE BEVERLY HILLBILLIES"

1. Who played the Drysdales?
2. According to the theme song, how did Jed discover oil?
3. Who or what was Claude?
4. In what bank did Jed Clampett keep his $60 million?
5. Who created the series, which ran for nine years?
6. On *The Bob Cummings Show,* she played Pamela Livingston. What part did she play on *Hillbillies,* and who is she?
7. Who provided the trained animals frequently employed on the show?
8. What oil company bought the Clampett's Osark property?
9. Who was Jethro's mother and sister?
10. Of Max Baer, Donna Douglas, Irene Ryan, and Buddy Ebsen, who hails from Baywood, Louisiana?

72. ON LOCATION

1. What was Charlie Weaver's hometown?
2. Who lived at the Broken Wheel Ranch?
3. What was the name of the traveling circus featured on *Circus Boy?*
4. Name the mountain on *Here Come the Brides.*
5. In what POW camp (stalag) were *Hogan's Heroes* held prisoner?
6. Name the Arthur Godfrey singer who hailed from Hawaii.
7. Actors Phil Carey and Warren Stevens romped in an adventure series set in India. Name it.
8. Where was *The Monroes* set?
9. Hong Kong served as the backdrop for a Rod Taylor series. What did he do for a living in it?
10. Which of the fifty states was depicted in *State Trooper?*

73. COURTROOM QUIZ

Match the lawyer with the series in which he
practiced.

1. Paul Drake
2. John Egan
3. Ben Caldwell
4. Danny Paterno
5. Paul Bryan
6. Bentley Gregg
7. Oliver Wendell
   Douglas
8. George Baxter
9. Bradley J. Stevens
10. Paul Simms

a. *Perry Mason*
b. *I Married Joan*
c. *Arrest and Trial*
d. *Bachelor Father*
e. *Judd for the Defense*
f. *The Paul Lynde Show*

g. *Hazel*
h. *Green Acres*
i. *Run For Your Life*
j. *Owen Marshall:
   Counselor at Law*

74. "THE DICK VAN DYKE SHOW"

1. Who was Herman Glimpsher?
2. What was Laura's maiden name?
3. Who created the popular sitcom?
4. What did Jerry Helper do for a living?
5. Dick's brother, Jerry, appeared in what role?
6. In what New York suburb did the Petries live?
7. Who played their milkman?
8. In one episode, who played a gangster by the name of Calvada?
9. How many seasons did the series run?
10. What was the relationship between Mel Cooley and Alan Brady?

75. CASTING CALL

Name the TV series in which each group of actors appeared.

1. Larry Ward, Jack Elam, Chad Everett, and Mike Greene
2. George O'Hanlon, Remo Pisani, Harry Guardino, and Gary Merrill
3. Peter Haskell, Elizabeth Allen, Leslie Nielsen, and Eleanor Parker
4. Steve Harmon, George Ives, Roger Smith, and Richard X. Slattery
5. Elinor Donahue, Mark Goddard, John McGiver, and Andrea Sacino
6. Will Hutchins, Sandy Baron, Michael Constantine, and Pamela Rodgers
7. Christopher George, Gary Raymond, Justin Tarr, and Hans Gudegast
8. Huntz Hall, Mike Mazurki, Marvin Kaplan, and Dean Jones
9. Michael Callan, Patricia Harty, Bryan O'Byrne, and Jack Collins
10. Lee Patterson, Diane McBain, Van Williams, and Troy Donahue

76. RELATIVELY SPEAKING

Name the TV series in which the following were related.
1. Jim Backus as Natalie Schafer's husband.
2. Gale Gordon as Bob Sweeney's brother.
3. Cathleen Nesbitt as William Windom's mother.
4. Don DeFore as Cathy Lewis' brother.
5. Florida Friebus as Frank Faylen's wife.
6. Paul Lynde as Agnes Moorehead's brother.
7. Barbara Hershey as Kevin Schultz's sister.
8. Brian Kelly as Tommy Norden's father.
9. James Garner as Jack Kelly's brother.
10. Thelma Carpenter as Tracy Reed's mother.

77. MOUSEKETEER MATCH

Match the first name of the *Micky Mouse Club* Mouseketeer with the last name.

1. Darlene
2. Sharon
3. Annette
4. Tommy
5. Cubby
6. Cheryl
7. Doreen
8. Karen
9. Bobby
10. Lonnie

a. Cole
b. O'Brien
c. Gillespie
d. Burgess
e. Tracey
f. Burr
g. Pendleton
h. Baird
i. Funicello
j. Holleridge

78. "THE UNTOUCHABLES"

1. Where was the series set?
2. Which federal agent did Jerry Paris portray?
3. Who collaborated with Eliot Ness on the original book, *The Untouchables?*
4. The pilot was aired on what anthology?
5. What villain did actor Bruce Gordon play?
6. Who was Ness' Indian-blooded accomplice?
7. How many seasons did the show run?
8. What character actor played Ness' boss, District Attorney Beecher Asbury?
9. Who provided the show's theme song?
10. What was Eliot's wife's name?

79. EMMY TEST

1. *Pantomime Quiz* with Mike Stokey won as "Most Popular Television Program" on the first awards show. What was the year?
2. Which was the first daytime serial to win an Emmy?
3. Translate N.A.T.A.S.
4. Who won more Emmys—Don Knotts, Milton Berle, or Lucille Ball?
5. What situation comedy swept the 1963-64 awards show?
6. What was the first situation comedy to win?
7. Who was the first black actor to win in the "Best Actor" category?
8. Name the early kiddie show that was the recipient of the first Emmy for children's programming.
9. In what general category did *Gunsmoke* win its first award (1957)?
10. What year was the first "International Award" given?

80. SOAP CITIES

Match the locale with the soap opera.

1. Oakdale	a.	*Search for Tomorrow*
2. Springfield	b.	*Days of Our Lives*
3. Montichello	c.	*As the World Turns*
4. Henderson	d.	*The Young and the Restless*
5. Woodbridge	e.	*The Guiding Light*
6. Bay City	f.	*All My Children*
7. Rosehill	g.	*The Secret Storm*
8. Salem	h.	*The Edge of Night*
9. Pine Valley	i.	*Love of Life*
10. Genoa City	j.	*Another World*

81. PAUSE FOR A COMMERCIAL

With what product would you associate the following slogans?
1. "Dishgusted, dishgusted, dishgusted."
2. "Get that good coffee feeling."
3. "———— battles Dirty Sludge and Blackie Carbon."
4. "Less irritating to the nose and throat."
5. "20,000 filter traps."
6. "Mildness is a pleasure with ————."
7. "Ask the man for ————."
8. "Why don't you pick me up and smoke me sometime?"
9. "———— tower of power."
10. "Light up a ————, it's light-up time."

82. "SESAME STREET"

1. Who created the Muppets?
2. What is David's ambition?
3. Name the neighborhood's friendly robot.
4. What day of the week is reserved for the retarded child?
5. Who's inside the Big Bird getup?
6. What is Oscar's official residence?
7. What character enjoyed a Top Ten record hit?
8. Who owns the candy store?
9. What PBS entity produces the show?
10. What's special about Mr. Snuffleupagus?

83. JOHNNY CARSON

1. Who composed "Johnny's Theme" for *The Tonight Show?*
2. What was the first game show he hosted?
3. On whose variety show did Carson serve as a comedy writer during the fifties?
4. What's Carson's brother's first name?
5. Which of Carson's characters is capable of rendering the answer to an unasked question?
6. What's his home state?
7. What is Carson's avocation?
8. Who was his first *Tonight Show* orchestra leader?
9. Whom did Carson replace as host of *Who Do You Trust?*
10. What happened to Herbert Buckingham Khaury on *The Tonight Show?*

84. VIDEOSYNCRASIES

Match the two performers who have *something* in common and explain the similarity.

1. Jerry Van Dyke
2. Richard Chamberlain
3. George O'Hanlon
4. Lee Tracy
5. Will Hutchins
6. Stanley Andrews
7. Raymond Massey
8. George Maharis
9. David Steinberg
10. Art Baker

a. Lloyd Nolan
b. Wayde Preston
c. Fred Gwynne
d. Ronald Reagan
e. Jack Smith
f. Richard Boone
g. Pete Seeger
h. Glenn Corbett
i. Tom D'Andrea
j. Robert Culp

85. TV MOVIES

1. What was the setting of *The Glass House?*
2. Who played Hal Holbrook's lover in *That Certain Summer?*
3. What social problem was depicted in *Go Ask Alice?*
4. Who played the leads in *Goodbye Charlie?*
5. What role did Billy Dee Williams play in *Brian's Song?*
6. During what period did *The Snow Goose* take place?
7. Who portrayed President John F. Kennedy on *The Missiles of October?*
8. Jan-Michael Vincent starred as a Marine recruit in this *ABC Movie of the Week* aired in 1970. Name it.
9. Who wrote the title music for the CBS TV movie *Sunshine?*
10. Who portrayed the gruff owner of a small-town delicatessen in *A Storm in Summer?*

86. "SERGEANT BILKO"

1. What did Barbella, Henshaw, and Fender have in common?
2. Name the Academy Award-winning actor who was the series' technical advisor.
3. What was Bilko's favorite nightclub in Roseville?
4. Fort Baxter was the comedy's first locale. What was the second?
5. Who was the original sponsor?
6. What were the platoon's "Four Freedoms"?
7. Who was Ernie's girlfriend?
8. What role did Hope Sansberry play?
9. Bet you can't remember Ernie's Army serial number.
10. When the series first went on the air, against what powerhouse was it scheduled?

87. GAME PLAN

Match the game shows which featured the same host, and then name him.

1. *Beat the Clock*
2. *College Bowl*
3. *Tic Tac Dough*
4. *Queen For a Day*
5. *Haggis Baggis*
6. *The Price Is Right*
7. *Earn Your
    Vacation*
8. *Songs for Sale*
9. *Mother's Day*
10. *Concentration*

a. *Twenty-One*
b. *Place the Face*
c. *Make a Face*
d. *To Tell the Truth*
e. *Password*
f. *Laugh Line*
g. *I've Got a Secret*
h. *Your First Impression*
i. *Truth or Consequences*
j. *Who Do You Trust?*

88. "STAR TREK"

1. State the ranks of Kirk, Scotty, Uhura, Sulu, and Chekov.
2. What was the *Enterprise*'s nurse's name and who portrayed the role?
3. How many seasons did it run and how many episodes were filmed?
4. What was the *Enterprise*'s registration number?
5. Which animation company filmed the "cartoon" version?
6. What are *Star Trek* aficionados called?
7. Who created the series?
8. What was the *Star Trek* counterpart of a gun called?
9. According to the opening narration, the solar mission was to last how many years?
10. In what century was the series set?

89. THAT FAMILIAR FACE

Identify the actor or actress who appeared as a regular in each trio of TV series.

1. *Gomer Pyle, U.S.M.C./That Girl/It's a Man's World*
2. *Overland Trail/Checkmate/The Virginian*
3. *Gunsmoke/Hawk/Riverboat*
4. *Lost in Space/Lassie/Petticoat Junction*
5. *The Life of Riley/Cavalcade of Stars/American Scene Magazine*
6. *The Charlie Farrell Show/Leave It to Beaver/The Mothers-In-Law*
7. *Our Miss Brooks/Slattery's People/The Real McCoys*
8. *Thicker Than Water/Bourbon Street Beat/The Big Valley*
9. *The Good Guys/The Many Loves of Dobie Gillis/Gilligan's Island*
10. *The Garry Moore Show/Bewitched/Mr. Peepers*

90. WOMEN OF THE WEST

Match the actress with the Western in which she appeared.

1. Sallie Brophy
2. Diana Douglas
3. Jeanette Nolan
4. Gail Davis
5. Fran Ryan
6. Gloria Winters
7. Diane Brewster
8. Anna Lisa
9. Audrey Totter
10. Linda Evans

a. *The Cowboys*
b. *Maverick*
c. *The Big Valley*
d. *Buckskin*
e. *Cimarron City*
f. *Gunsmoke*
g. *Hotel de Paree*
h. *Black Saddle*
i. *Sky King*
j. *Annie Oakley*

91. PLEASE STAND BY

1. Brian Donlevy played Steve Mitchell, a suave soldier of fortune, on what show?
2. What do the initials I.M.F. mean?
3. Name the pretty guardian of the three *Let's Make a Deal* doors.
4. Whom did actor Byron Foulger replace as co-engineer of the Hooterville Cannonball?
5. There are approximately 700 of them in the United States today. What are they?
6. According to a 1975 TV-viewing survey of Americans, Canadians, and Japanese, who watches television the most?
7. Stu Bergman (*Search for Tomorrow*) owned a used-car lot. Name it.
8. What kind of animal was the cartoon character, Rocky?
9. Dorothy Provine flopped in two consecutive Warner Brothers series. (In one she also flapped.) Name them.
10. Who was *Captain Video*'s evil foe?

92. "MAKE ROOM FOR DADDY"

1. Who was the Williams' maid?
2. Sherry Jackson played Danny's eldest daughter until Terry went off to college. Who played her after she graduated?
3. In what profession was Kathy engaged when she met Danny?
4. An adorable little Chinese girl appeared in several segments as Linda's friend Chou Lee. Who played the Oriental?
5. What role did William Demarest play?
6. Where did Danny Williams work?
7. Besides Mr. Thomas, who else used his first name as his character monicker?
8. Who played Uncle Tunoose?
9. Name the Williams' elevator operator.
10. Who played Charlie and Bunny Halper?

93. GOOD COMPANY

If you're a credits-watcher, you'll be able to match the production companies with the people who head them.

1. Marterto
2. Peekskill Enterprises
3. Clerow
4. Mark VII, Ltd.
5. Four Star Television
6. Jemmin
7. Gomalco
8. Arwin
9. Talent Associates
10. Daisy Productions

a. George Gobel
b. Flip Wilson
c. Jackie Gleason
d. Marlo Thomas
e. Danny Thomas
f. David Susskind
g. Jack Webb
h. Doris Day
i. Bill Cosby
j. Dick Powell

94. "GET SMART!"

1. Who created the secret agent show spoof?
2. What was the plastic dome used for private conversations called?
3. Where was the series set?
4. What character did Robert Karvalas play?
5. Who was Agent K-13?
6. How many digits did Don Adams dial on the pay phone in the opening film?
7. What company produced the program?
8. Who was the villainous head of KAOS, and who played him?
9. Who played 99's mother?
10. Of a Sunbeam, Triumph, and MG, which did Max drive?

95. NETWORK NOSTALGIA: ABC

1. Who is Director of Internal Medicine at *General Hospital?*
2. Who was the official *Voice of Firestone* conductor?
3. *Nightlife,* the network's short-lived answer to *The Tonight Show,* boasted what musical conductor?
4. What was Kookie's full name?
5. When and where did the network enter the TV business?
6. Who played *Wyatt Earp?*
7. Name the popular conversationalist who began his talk-show career as a 1969 summer replacement.
8. Of Huntley and Brinkley, who worked in the ABC News department for a number of years?
9. Who was Joey Bishop's late-night talk-show sidekick?
10. In 1969 the network scheduled *The Music Scene* and *The New People* back-to-back. What was unusual about these two Monday night programs?

96. MILTON BERLE

1. Who played Miltie's heckling foil, Irving Spritzer?
2. Berle's attempted comeback in the sixties featured two young singers. Name them.
3. How many overall-clad men sang the Texaco opening song, "Oh, we're the men of Texaco. We work from Maine to Mexico . . ."?
4. Who else was Berle referring to when he said, "We both work for the same boss—Sky Chief"?
5. Ruth Gilbert played Berle's love-struck secretary, Maxine. Who played his agent?
6. After Texaco dropped its sponsorship in 1953, what company took over?
7. At Uncle Miltie's peak, what was the percentage of TV sets tuned to him?
8. Can you remember any of the guest stars on his very first show, September 14, 1948?
9. Within $1,000, estimate the budget of one of Berle's early *Texaco Star Theaters?*
10. Name the female comedy scribe who was a member of Berle's writing staff.

97. ENGLISH CHANNEL

1. Name the show in which the hero and heroine took orders from a person named "Mother."
2. What was Patrick McGoohan's role on *Secret Agent?*
3. On *Fair Exchange,* who portrayed the British father-and-daughter complement?
4. Who played the title role in *Man in a Suitcase?*
5. On her situation comedy, Shirley MacLaine played an on-the-go career woman. What was her profession?
6. Who was Simon Templar better known as?
7. *Upstairs, Downstairs* was a regular feature of what PBS anthology?
8. On what science-fiction series was the Supreme Headquarters Alien Defense Organization (SHADO) featured?
9. Who played TV's *Sir Francis Drake?*
10. Who was known as "Number Six"?

98. VIDEO VARIETY

Match the performer with the variety show in which he or she appeared.

1. Jimmy Nelson   a. *The Ken Murray Show*
2. Billy Williams
   Quartet   b. *The George Gobel Show*
3. Laurie Anders   c. *The Original Amateur Hour*
4. Frank Nelson   d. *Texaco Star Theater*
5. Audrey Meadows   e. *The Garry Moore Show*
6. Phyllis Kirk   f. *Your Show of Shows*
7. Dennis James   g. *Arthur Godfrey and His Friends*
8. Janette Davis   h. *The Bob and Ray Show*
9. Ken Carson   i. *The Red Buttons Show*
10. Phyllis Avery   j. *The Jack Benny Show*

99. ARE WE ON?

1. The characters on *Follow the Sun* shared what profession?
2. Who played Loren Greene's assistants on *Griff?*
3. For what government agency did Alexander Mundy work?
4. In what part of 1870's America was *Laramie* set?
5. Who played the *Maverick* brothers' cousin?
6. Gary Lockwood's *Lieutenant* served in what service branch?
7. Where did *Banacek* live?
8. What did *Star Trek* and *Riverboat* have in common?
9. Name the series which depicted stories of the 918th Bombardment Group of the 8th Air Force during World War II.
10. David McLean played a disabled Civil War veteran in what short-lived series?
11. Do you recall Mr. Magoo's first name?

ANSWERS

QUIZ 1

1. *The Long, Long Trailer* and *Forever, Darling*
2. Joan Blondell
3. Dick Martin of Rowan and Martin fame
4. *Constitution*
5. Irma
6. Doris Singleton
7. Bob Carroll, Jr., Madelyn Pugh, and Jess Oppenheimer
8. Barney Kurtz
9. Sherman Bagley
10. 846 North Gower Street

QUIZ 2

1. c
2. e
3. f
4. i
5. j
6. a
7. h
8. b
9. g
10. d

QUIZ 3

1. A changing kaleidoscope within the CBS eye
2. "The knight can move in eight different directions at any given time. You never know where the attack is coming from."
3. Proctor and Gamble
4. Charles Collingwood
5. Richard Bradford
6. Seventh
7. Theocradus Kojakzakilas
8. William Golden, in 1951
9. Greg Morris and Peter Lupus
10. Sam, the bartender at the Longbranch

QUIZ 4

1. Sarah
2. Bee's friend, Clara Edwards
3. Beasley
4. Howard Morris
5. Jackson and Oliver, respectively
6. The Darlings
7. Employer; he owned the filling station
8. 14 Maple Street, Mayberry
9. Rose
10. Ellie Walker, the druggist's daughter

QUIZ 5

1. Helen
2. Her husband's helicopter was shot down in Vietnam
3. The leads were played by real-life husbands and wives
4. Patty Toma
5. Each portrayed a wife of Andy Griffith
6. Wendell Corey's
7. *Topper*
8. Patricia Harty
9. Jane
10. Joey Bishop

QUIZ 6

1. c, *The Gale Storm Show*
2. f, *The Danny Thomas Show*
3. j, *Topper*
4. a, *Lassie*
5. i, *Circus Boy*
6. h, *Dragnet*
7. b, *Our Miss Brooks*
8. g, *I Love Lucy*
9. e, *Amos 'n' Andy*
10. d, *Rin Tin Tin*

QUIZ 7

1. Michael Francis O'Casey; William Frawley
2. Tim Considine, Don Grady, and Stanley Livingston
3. Katie, played by Tina Cole
4. Dawn Lyn
5. Saxophone
6. Uncle Charlie
7. Three
8. Stanley and Barry Livingston
9. Don Fedderson
10. ABC and CBS

QUIZ 8

1. Wrestling
2. Dizzy Dean and Buddy Blattner; later Pee-wee Reese
3. ABC
4. Charles Goren
5. Dale Robertson
6. Saturday night fights announcer
7. Bill Nimmo
8. 1956
9. Track and field
10. Wrestling

QUIZ 9

1. Defiance Castle in Galahad Glen
2. *Rocky and His Friends*
3. *Beany and Cecil*
4. George Jetson
5. Riverdale High School
6. Pertwee; voice of Paul Lynde
7. *Underdog*
8. Melody and Valerie
9. *Heckle and Jeckle*
10. Nell

QUIZ 10

1. b, Not a Red Skelton character
2. b, Not associated with *The Tonight Show*
3. e, Did not portray a lawyer
4. c, Not in U.S. Army
5. a, Not a rotating star on *Alcoa-Goodyear Playhouse*
6. e, Leonard Rosenman did not compose the theme
7. a, Did not play a TV Ellery Queen
8. d, Not a *Sesame Street* character
9. e, Not a Flying A production (Gene Autry's company)
10. d, Regulars had nothing to do with *The Dick Van Dyke Show*

QUIZ 11

1. e
2. c
3. g
4. j
5. h
6. d
7. f
8. i
9. b
10. a

QUIZ 12

1. Johnny Washbrook; *My Friend Flicka*
2. Barbara Bel Geddes; *I Remember Mama*
3. Yul Brynner; *Anna and the King*
4. Leon Ames; *Father of the Bride*
5. Patricia Harty; *Blondie*
6. Christopher Connelly; *Paper Moon*
7. Wayne Rogers; *M*A*S*H*
8. Manuel Padilla, Jr.; *Tarzan*
9. Ralph Taeger; *Hondo*
10. David Carradine; *Shane*

QUIZ 13

1. Jim Nabors
2. *The Snows of Kilimanjaro*
3. *The Constant Wife*
4. Howard K. Smith
5. *Hot L Baltimore*
6. Evelyn Margaret Ay
7. Gerald S. Ford, on November 9, 1975
8. *Fame Is the Name of the Game*
9. A Brooklyn Dodgers–Philadelphia Phillies baseball game
10. Dwight D. Eisenhower, January 19, 1955

QUIZ 14

1. Al Caiola
2. Saturday
3. Virginia City
4. Fourteen
5. Jamie
6. Sea captain and storekeeper
7. Architecture
8. Lorne Greene
9. Chevrolet
10. Six

QUIZ 15

1. *Gunsmoke*
2. India
3. James Hong
4. *Cowboy in Africa*
5. Walter Brennan
6. *Soldiers of Fortune*
7. Dermot Walsh
8. Thomas Mitchell
9. In and around the Iron Curtain countries
10. Merle Oberon

QUIZ 16

1. d
2. g
3. h
4. e
5. f
6. i
7. b
8. c
9. j
10. a

QUIZ 17

1. Dodge City, later Tombstone
2. *Hootenanny*
3. Rosey Grier
4. James Komack
5. A large New Mexico ranch owned by the Garrett family
6. A gambling ship
7. Accountant-turned-spy
8. *Dan Raven*
9. *Four Just Men*
10. Shoe salesman

QUIZ 18

1. *PT 73*
2. County General
3. Wednesday Afternoon Fine Arts League
4. Fred Flintstone and Barney Rubble
5. Pokey's master was Porky
6. Mrs. Livingston
7. Joey Newton
8. Commissioner Gordon
9. Kitty Russell
10. Mockingbird Heights

QUIZ 19

1. c
2. e
3. h
4. f
5. g
6. b
7. i
8. j
9. a
10. d

QUIZ 20

1. David
2. Man, woman, birth, death, and infinity
3. Dr. Maggie Graham
4. Harry Landers
5. Sam Jaffe and Bettye Ackerman
6. James E. Moser
7. Kanavaras
8. Monday
9. Bing Crosby
10. Dr. Allan M. Warner

QUIZ 21

1. Willie Best
2. Chicago
3. American history
4. Peggy Fair; Gail Fisher
5. Horace Stewart
6. *Love Thy Neighbor*
7. Beulah
8. Barney
9. Rupert Crosse
10. Jones

QUIZ 22

1. d
2. f
3. a
4. g
5. j
6. c
7. i
8. e
9. b
10. h

QUIZ 23

1. September, 1955
2. Children
3. "She Loves You" and "I Wanna Hold Your Hand"
4. Lincoln-Mercury division of the Ford Motor Company
5. $50,000
6. All appeared on the first show—June 20, 1948
7. 23 years
8. Sylvia
9. Julia Meade
10. They were all driven off the air by Sullivan's high ratings.

QUIZ 24

1. *Laugh-In*
2. *The Beverly Hillbillies*
3. Edward R. Murrow
4. Steve Allen on *What's My Line?*
5. *Captain Kangaroo*
6. Ricky Ricardo on *I Love Lucy*
7. Red Skelton
8. Peter Potter on *Jukebox Jury*
9. Sergeant Preston
10. Molly Goldberg

QUIZ 25

1. a
2. d
3. h
4. f
5. i
6. b
7. j
8. e
9. g
10. c

QUIZ 26

1. True
2. True
3. False
4. True
5. False
6. False
7. True
8. False
9. True
10. True

QUIZ 27

1. Maudie Prickett
2. Tutor St. John Quincy
3. Mrs. Manicotti
4. Gypsy Rose Lee
5. Bluebird Diner
6. Hillary Brooke
7. Pahoo-Ka-Ta-Wah
8. Dobie Gillis; Steve Franken, Tuesday Weld, and Dwayne Hickman
9. Dick Wesson
10. Valentine Farrow of *Valentine's Day*

QUIZ 28

1. *Jeopardy*
2. *Concentration*
3. *To Tell the Truth*
4. *Queen For a Day* or *Strike It Rich*
5. *Mike Stokey's Pantomime Quiz*
6. *Beat the Clock*
7. *Hollywood Squares* or *Tic Tac Dough*
8. *Feather Your Nest*
9. *The Sky's the Limit*
10. *Masquerade Party*

QUIZ 29

1. d
2. f
3. h
4. j
5. i
6. a
7. b
8. e or c
9. g
10. c o r e

QUIZ 30

1. William Schallert
2. Frank Ballinger
3. *Mrs. G. Goes to College*
4. Mr. Lucky
5. Robert Francis Logan as J. R. Hale
6. Peter Breck
7. Sunrise
8. Car racing—*Straightaway*
9. Johnny Wayne and Frank Shuster
10. Don Ameche

QUIZ 31

1. Jack E. Stewart and Paul Wallace
2. Burgess Vale
3. Louise
4. Fronk
5. Cameron Brooks on *Window on Main Street*
6. Printing
7. Radio series
8. The Davises
9. Ford
10. Football

QUIZ 32

1. Helen Keller
2. Gore Vidal
3. *The Days of Wine and Roses*
4. *Playhouse 90*
5. Delbert Mann
6. *Patterns*
7. Bette Davis
8. Mountain McClintock
9. *Playhouse 90*
10. George Voskovec and Joseph Sweeney

QUIZ 33

1. d, Eve Arden
2. f, Joan Caulfield
3. a, Marion Lorne
4. g, Bea Benadaret
5. h, Rose Marie
6. j, Brian Keith
7. c, Robert Culp
8. b, James Hampton
9. i, Michael Constantine
10. e, Jay North

QUIZ 34

1. Lawrence Spivak
2. To help TV set owners check the perform-
   ance of their receivers by providing circles,
   definition wedges, and shading gradations
   with which to judge reception and make
   tuning adjustments
3. She was a *Roller Derby* favorite
4. 190,000
5. John Cameron Swayze
6. The Rose Bowl (Michigan *vs*. USC, 49-0)
7. "It's Howdy Doody time. It's Howdy Doody
   time. Bob Smith and Howdy, too, say
   howdy-do to you!"
8. The silver bullet
9. Jack Barry
10. Topper

QUIZ 35

1. Arthur Godfrey—*Arthur Godfrey and His Friends* and *Arthur Godfrey's Talent Scouts*
2. George S. Kaufman
3. Pianist-singer Bob Howard
4. Dumont
5. *Super Circus*
6. Olsen and Johnson
7. Goodman Ace and his wife Jane
8. Cooking
9. *Admiral Broadway Revue*
10. Arturo Toscanini

QUIZ 36

1. *Tom Corbett, Space Cadet*
2. *The Rootie Kazootie Club*
3. Chesterfield
4. *What's My Line?*
5. Bob Hope
6. Garry Moore
7. West Virginia
8. The May Company
9. Jack Bailey
10. They were both about newspapermen

QUIZ 37

1. *Amos 'n' Andy*
2. Ralph Edwards
3. High school principal
4. Loco
5. Both appeared on *The Jack Benny Show*
6. Peggy McCay and Bonnie Bartlett
7. 40
8. George Gershwin
9. Captain Braddock
10. *Down You Go*

QUIZ 38

1. Richard Rodgers
2. "Cry" by Johnnie Ray
3. Domestic Court
4. *The Adventures of Ozzie and Harriet*
5. Carlton Arms Apartments on East 57th Street in New York City
6. Ford Foundation
7. Snodgrass
8. "The William Tell Overture"
9. Darby
10. J. R. Boone, played by Ross Ford

QUIZ 39

1. *The Ford 50th Anniversary Show*
2. The Bronx
3. Katie
4. Robinson
5. Jack Paar
6. Hoagy Carmichael
7. Charita Bauer as Bert Bauer
8. Adolphe Menjou
9. Louise Beavers and Amanda Randolph
10. Lucille Ball's for *My Favorite Husband*

QUIZ 40

1. Tennessee, state, Raised, b'ar (bear), frontier
2. Julius Caesar
3. Betty Hutton
4. *Disneyland*
5. Ames
6. John Eldredge
7. Anagrams
8. Rusty "B" Company
9. Don Haggerty
10. Hilda Crocker

QUIZ 41

1. *Matinee Theater*
2. Manufacturers Trust Company
3. Water Commissioner of Summerfield
4. 60,000 acres
5. (Aunt) Gus Miller
6. Bulova
7. Treasure House
8. Mr. Darling and Captain Hook
9. Lawrence Welk
10. Judy Garland

QUIZ 42

1. *On Trial*
2. Dean Martin and Jerry Lewis
3. A New York hotel lobby newsstand
4. *Circus Boy*
5. Chet Huntley and David Brinkley
6. Susanna Pomeroy
7. Betty Furness for Westinghouse—$100,000-a-year salary
8. Lofty Craig
9. *As the World Turns;* he played Grandpa Hughes
10. Dick Powell

QUIZ 43

1. *American Bandstand*
2. Johnny Western
3. Bernardo
4. *My Friend Flicka*
5. *I Love Lucy* to *The Lucille Ball–Desi Arnaz Show*
6. Charlie
7. Tony Martinez
8. Brooklyn Dodgers
9. Gumby
10. Miss Clairol

QUIZ 44

1. $264,000
2. *The Rifleman*
3. Josh Randall, played by Steve McQueen on *Wanted—Dead or Alive*
4. *Rough Riders*
5. Vincent Price
6. Mother's
7. Betty White
8. Fred Davis and Jack Lescoulie
9. Colonel Steve Canyon
10. Ed Wynn

QUIZ 45

1. *Meet the Press*
2. Greenwich Village in New York City
3. Darren McGavin
4. "Eye of the Beholder"
5. Warner Anderson
6. Sara Seeger
7. *The Untouchables*
8. Margaret
9. *The Detectives*
10. Mayor LaTrivia

QUIZ 46

1. Porter
2. *SurfSide 6*
3. Water closet, a/k/a "WC," a/k/a bathroom
4. Lucille Ball and Desi Arnaz
5. Betty Rubble
6. Milton Berle
7. *Naked City*
8. *Happy*
9. Boris Karloff
10. Both created by Jess Oppenheimer

QUIZ 47

1. Palomino
2. Bob Cummings'
3. James
4. Toody and Muldoon; *Car 54, Where Are You?*
5. James Whitmore
6. Bob McGrath
7. Jim Hardie in *Tales of Wells Fargo*
8. *Ripcord*
9. A father-and-son team of lawyers—Lawrence and Kenneth Preston
10. *The Investigators* and *Longstreet*

QUIZ 48

1. *The Virginian*
2. *Appleby*
3. Dickens and Fenster
4. 53rd
5. Jack Lord in *Stoney Burke*
6. Westfield
7. Alice and Duncan MacRoberts
8. *Wagon Train*
9. Vic Damone
10. Europe during World War II

QUIZ 49

1. Paul O'Keefe
2. Shady Rest
3. Burgess Meredith
4. Elizabeth Taylor
5. *The Doctors*
6. Mr. Cooper
7. Dan O'Herlihy
8. *The Rifleman*
9. Lois, Rusty, and Terry
10. Granville

QUIZ 50

1. Jimmy Boyd
2. Lawyer
3. Richard Crenna; *Slattery's People*
4. Irna Phillips
5. United Network for Command of Law Enforcement
6. The Technological Hierarchy for the Removal of Undesirables and the Subjugation of Humanity
7. Charles Boyer, Gig Young, David Niven, and Robert Coote, with Gladys Cooper
8. Gateman, Goodbury and Graves, a funeral parlor
9. Craig Stevens; *Mr. Broadway*
10. *Flipper*

QUIZ 51

1. PZR 317
2. Two years
3. *The Wild, Wild West*
4. Sheldon Leonard
5. *Please Don't Eat the Daisies*
6. *Petticoat Junction*
7. Esso
8. Dean Martin
9. Kenneth Washington
10. *Gidget,* played by Sally Field

QUIZ 52

1. *The Green Hornet*
2. On Robinwood Lane in Southampton, New York
3. T. Hewett Edward Cat
4. *The Newlywed Game* and *The Dating Game*
5. *ABC Stage 67*
6. Five seconds
7. Everett Dirksen
8. Ruth McDevitt
9. *Days of Our Lives*
10. *Family Affair*

QUIZ 53

1. Hildy and Joey
2. Both
3. Robert T. Ironside
4. Joseph Campanella
5. *The Jonathan Winters Show*
6. *Cimarron Strip*
7. Potion
8. Wayne Maunder
9. The Convent San Tanco in Puerto Rico
10. *Gentle Ben*

QUIZ 54

1. ABC's *One Life to Live*
2. Richard Steele
3. Glen Campbell
4. *Crime Magazine* and *People Magazine*
5. Mill Valley, California
6. Lurene Tuttle
7. *Playboy After Dark*
8. Phyllis Diller's
9. The San Joaquin Valley of California in the 1870's
10. Billy Barnes

QUIZ 55

1. Jim
2. Jan-Michael Vincent
3. Jack
4. Miyoshi Umeki
5. David Victor
6. Martin
7. Captain Adam Greer, played by Tige Andrews
8. *Movie of the Week*
9. Associate Professor of Surgery at the College of Medicine
10. *The Debbie Reynolds Show*

QUIZ 56

1. Taos
2. Nanette Fabray and Louis Quinn
3. *The Partridge Family*
4. "Only A Man"
5. The Agency to Prevent Evil
6. Michael Hughes
7. Chet Huntley
8. Phone number of the American Embassy in Paris, setting of a George Hamilton series
9. Carole Shelley and Monica Evans
10. *Nancy*

QUIZ 57

1. 5,000
2. Phoebe and Charles Tyler
3. Dick Van Dyke
4. *Getting Together*
5. Judy Graubart
6. *Owen Marshall: Counselor At Law*
7. *The Chicago Teddy Bears*
8. Johnny Mann
9. David Wayne
10. Harry Guardino

QUIZ 58

1. 4077
2. Radames Pera
3. Cavender
4. Five: Lance, Kevin, Grant, Delilah, and Michelle
5. 51
6. Anne Jeffreys
7. *Banyon*
8. *Ghost Story*
9. *The Paul Lynde Show*
10. Christine Belford

QUIZ 59

1. *Search*
2. *Lotsa Luck*
3. College coeds—Brenda and Susan
4. Robert Clary
5. France, during World War II
6. Ernesta and Gwen
7. 28 years
8. Benjamin
9. Bill Bixby as *The Magician*
10. Amanda Bonner, played by Blythe Danner

QUIZ 60

1. Fred
2. *Cyborg*
3. 332 West 64th Street, New York City
4. Rosemary Prinz
5. Owned a hardware store
6. Roddy McDowall
7. Four: Truckie, Doobie, TJ, and Boo
8. I.N.S.
9. Harry S. Truman Memorial High School in St. Louis, Missouri
10. The thirties

QUIZ 61

1. Ja'net DuBois (Willona)
2. James Buchanan H.S.
3. *The Sting*
4. *Police Story*
5. Barbara Colby
6. *Calucci's Dept.*
7. *The Sonny Comedy Revue*
8. Zebec
9. Jeremiah, played by Cameron Mitchell
10. KONE-TV, Channel 1

QUIZ 62

1. d, *Medic*
2. f, *Dr. Hudson's Secret Journal*
3. h, *Dr. Christian*
4. i, *Peyton Place*
5. e, *Breaking Point*
6. b, *The Little People*
7. a, *Matt Lincoln*
8. j, *The Doctors and the Nurses*
9. g, *The Eleventh Hour*
10. c, *The Interns*

QUIZ 63

1. A Bulova clock showing the time
2. September, 1957
3. Atop the Empire State Building
4. *Somerset*
5. *Mr. Peepers*—Nancy's parents, and *Father Knows Best*—Margaret's folks
6. *The Rifleman*
7. It was one hour long
8. *The Virginian*
9. Sylvester L. ("Pat") Weaver
10. *Ninety Bristol Court*

QUIZ 64

1. Arlene Francis
2. Patti Page
3. Bing Crosby
4. Red Buttons or Gary Owens
5. Liberace
6. Dinah Shore
7. Tennessee Ernie Ford
8. Kate Smith
9. John Cameron Swayze
10. Carol Burnett

QUIZ 65

1. 704 Houser Street, Queens, New York
2. The McNabs, the Jeffersons, the Lorenzos
3. Carroll O'Connor
4. Billy Halop
5. Bob Hastings
6. Joey Stivic
7. Edith's cousin
8. According to Edith, Reverend Felcher; to Archie, Reverend Fletcher
9. *Til Death Us Do Part*
10. Meathead

QUIZ 66

1. j
2. d
3. h
4. b or e
5. e or b
6. g
7. f
8. a
9. c
10. i

QUIZ 67

1. 3
2. 2
3. 1
4. 9
5. 5
6. 10
7. 8
8. 6
9. 7
10. 4

QUIZ 68

1. Mayfield
2. Squirt
3. Miss Landers and Mrs. Rayburn
4. Gus, the fireman
5. Whitney
6. Grant Avenue Grammar School
7. Stephen Talbot
8. Six seasons, 234 episodes
9. Benjie
10. Frank Bank

QUIZ 69

1. e, *The Donna Reed Show*
2. g, *The Dennis O'Keefe Show*
3. a, *The Adventures of Tugboat Annie*
4. j, *Lancer*
5. i, *The Name of the Game*
6. b, *Perry Mason*
7. h, *Born Free*
8. f, *Bracken's World*
9. d, *My World and Welcome To It*
10. c, *Calucci's Dept.*

QUIZ 70

1. Rosemary DeCamp
2. "The Glea Girls"
3. Frank Fontaine
4. "That'll carry us through the night, but what'll we do in the morning?"
5. The announcer for Mother Fletcher's products
6. Sue Ane Langdon
7. Bensonhurst section of Brooklyn
8. June Taylor
9. Pert Kelton
10. Miami Beach, Florida

QUIZ 71

1. Raymond Bailey and Harriet MacGibbon
2. ". . . one day he was shootin' at some food and up through the ground came a-bubblin' crude . . . oil . . ."
3. Mrs. Drysdale's French poodle
4. The Commerce Bank of Beverly Hills
5. Paul Henning
6. Jane Hathaway; Nancy Kulp
7. Frank Inn
8. The OK Oil Company
9. Pearl and Jethrine Bodine
10. Donna Douglas

QUIZ 72

1. Mt. Idy, Ohio
2. Joey, Jim, Pete, and Fury
3. "Burke and Walsh"
4. Bridal Veil
5. Thirteen
6. Haleoke
7. *The 77th Bengal Lancers*
8. Wyoming
9. Newspaper correspondent
10. Nevada

QUIZ 73

1. a
2. c
3. e
4. j
5. i
6. d
7. h
8. g
9. b
10. f

QUIZ 74

1. Sally Rogers' occasional boyfriend, played by Bill Idelson
2. Mein
3. Carl Reiner
4. Dentist
5. Rob's brother, Stacy
6. New Rochelle, New York
7. Jerry Hausner
8. Sheldon Leonard; it was also the name of the production company
9. Five seasons; 158 episodes
10. They were brothers-in-law

QUIZ 75

1. *The Dakotas*
2. *The Reporter*
3. *Bracken's World*
4. *Mr. Roberts*
5. *Many Happy Returns*
6. *Hey, Landlord!*
7. *Rat Patrol*
8. *The Chicago Teddy Bears*
9. *Occasional Wife*
10. *SurfSide 6*

QUIZ 76

1. *Gilligan's Island*
2. *The Brothers*
3. *The Farmer's Daughter*
4. *Hazel*
5. *The Many Loves of Dobie Gillis*
6. *Bewitched*
7. *The Monroes*
8. *Flipper*
9. *Maverick*
10. *Barefoot in the Park*

QUIZ 77

1. c
2. h
3. i
4. a
5. b
6. j
7. e
8. g
9. d
10. f

QUIZ 78

1. In Chicago; Ness' office was Room 208 of the Federal Building
2. Martin Flaherty
3. Oscar Fraley
4. *Desilu Playhouse*
5. Frank Nitti, "The Enforcer"
6. William Youngfellow
7. Four; 114 episodes
8. Frank Wilcox
9. Nelson Riddle
10. Betty Anderson

QUIZ 79

1. 1949 for 1948 achievement
2. *The Doctors,* 1971
3. The National Academy of Television Arts and Sciences
4. Don Knotts; five Emmys
5. *The Dick Van Dyke Show*—five major awards
6. *The Life of Riley* (1949)
7. Bill Cosby
8. *Time For Beany*
9. "Best Dramatic Series With Continuing Characters"
10. 1962 for *War and Peace*

QUIZ 80

1. c
2. e
3. h
4. a
5. g
6. j
7. i
8. b
9. f
10. d

QUIZ 81

1. Lux Liquid
2. Maxwell House Coffee
3. Bardahl
4. Philip Morris
5. Viceroy
6. Pall Mall
7. Ballantine
8. Muriel cigars
9. Texaco
10. Lucky Strike

QUIZ 82

1. Jim Henson
2. To be a lawyer
3. Sam
4. Wednesday
5. Carroll Spinney
6. A trash can
7. Ernie for "Rubber Duckie"
8. Mr. Hooper
9. Children's Television Workshop
10. Only Big Bird sees him

QUIZ 83

1. Paul Anka
2. *Earn Your Vacation*
3. Red Skelton
4. Dick
5. Carnac
6. Nebraska
7. Magician
8. Skitch Henderson
9. Edgar Bergen
10. Better known as Tiny Tim, he got married

QUIZ 84

1. c, Starred in series with the word "car" in title
2. f, Played TV doctors
3. i, Next door neighbors of Chester A. Riley
4. a, Played Martin Kane, a TV private eye
5. b, Starred in TV versions of Randolph Scott Western movies: *Sugarfoot* and *Colt .45*
6. d, Hosts of *Death Valley Days*
7. j, Starred in series titled *I Spy;* 1955 and 1965
8. h, Shared the front seat of a Corvette with Martin Milner
9. g, Subjects of *Smothers Brothers Show* censorship
10. e, Hosted *You Asked For It*

QUIZ 85

1. Utah State Prison
2. Martin Sheen
3. Drug addiction
4. Patty Duke and Al Freeman
5. Football player Gale Sayers
6. World War II
7. William Devane
8. *Tribes*
9. John Denver
10. Peter Ustinov

QUIZ 86

1. All corporals
2. George Kennedy
3. The Paradise Bar and Grill
4. Camp Fremont in Grove City, California
5. Camel cigarettes
6. Bingo, poker, roulette, and dice
7. Joan Hogan
8. Nell Hall
9. 15042699
10. Milton Berle

QUIZ 87

1. d, Bud Collyer
2. e, Allen Ludden
3. a, Jack Barry
4. i, Jack Bailey
5. h, Dennis James
6. b, Bill Cullen
7. j, Johnny Carson
8. g, Steve Allen
9. f, Dick Van Dyke
10. c, Bob Clayton

QUIZ 88

1. Captain, Lieutenant Commander, Lieutenant, Lieutenant, and Ensign, respectively
2. Nurse Chapel; Majel Barrett
3. Three seasons; 76 episodes
4. NCC-1701
5. Filmation
6. Trekkies
7. Gene Roddenberry
8. Phaser
9. Five
10. 23rd

QUIZ 89

1. Ted Bessell
2. Doug McClure
3. Burt Reynolds
4. June Lockhart
5. Jackie Gleason
6. Richard Deacon
7. Richard Crenna
8. Richard Long
9. Bob Denver
10. Marion Lorne

QUIZ 90

1. d
2. a
3. g
4. j
5. f
6. i
7. b
8. h
9. e
10. c

QUIZ 91

1. *Dangerous Assignment*
2. Impossible Missions Force
3. Carole Merrill
4. Smiley Burnette
5. TV stations
6. Japanese
7. West Side Autos
8. Squirrel
9. *The Alaskans* and *The Roaring Twenties*
10. Tobor

QUIZ 92

1. Louise, played by Louise Beavers and Amanda Randolph
2. Penny Parker
3. Nursing
4. Ginny Tiu
5. Kathy's father
6. The Copa Club
7. Rusty Hamer
8. Hans Conried
9. Jose Jimenez (Bill Dana)
10. Sid Melton and Pat Carroll

QUIZ 93

1. e
2. c
3. b
4. g
5. j
6. i
7. a
8. h
9. f
10. d

QUIZ 94

1. Mel Brooks with Buck Henry
2. The cone of silence
3. Washington, D.C.
4. Larabee, the Chief's assistant
5. Fang, a dog
6. Three
7. Talent Associates
8. Siegfried; Bernie Kopell
9. Jane Dulo
10. Sunbeam

QUIZ 95

1. Dr. Steve Hardy
2. Howard Barlow
3. Elliot Lawrence
4. Gerald Lloyd Kookson III
5. August 10, 1948, with New York Station WJZ-TV, Channel 7
6. Hugh O'Brian
7. Dick Cavett
8. Chet Huntley
9. Regis Philbin
10. Each was 45 minutes in length

QUIZ 96

1. Irv Benson
2. Bobby Rydell and Donna Loren
3. Four
4. Bishop Fulton J. Sheen, his *Texaco Star Theater* competition
5. Fred Clark
6. Buick
7. Seventy-five percent
8. Pearl Bailey, Señor Wences, Smith and Dale, and Bill (Bojangles) Robinson
9. $15,000
10. Selma Diamond

QUIZ 97

1. *The Avengers*
2. John Drake
3. Judy Carne and Victor Madden
4. Richard Bradford
5. Photojournalist
6. *The Saint*
7. *Masterpiece Theatre*
8. *UFO*
9. Terence Morgan
10. *The Prisoner* played by Patrick McGoohan

QUIZ 98

1. d
2. f
3. a
4. j
5. h
6. i
7. b
8. g
9. e
10. c

QUIZ 99

1. Free-lance writing
2. Ben Murphy and Gracie Newcombe
3. S.I.A.
4. Wyoming territory
5. Roger Moore
6. U.S.M.C.
7. Boston
8. The *Enterprise*
9. *Twelve O'Clock High*
10. *Tate*
11. Quincy

PHOTO ALBUM

1. John Hamilton
2. Sam
3. Fred Clark and Larry Keating
4. Frank Smith
5. *Masquerade Party*
6. ABC
7. Martha; Mary Lansing
8. Pat Priest and Beverley Owen
9. Don Jose Bluster
10. Wladziu Valentino Liberace